R

QUARTZ

Also by Sasha taqʷšəblu LaPointe

Red Paint

ROSE
QUARTZ

poems

Sasha taqʷšəblu LaPointe

MILKWEED EDITIONS

Published 2023 by Milkweed Editions
Printed in the United States
Cover design by Mary Austin Speaker
Cover art by Fumi Mini Nakamura
Author photo by Bridget McGee Houchins

Library of Congress Cataloging-in-Publication Data

Names: LaPointe, Sasha taqwšeblu, author.
Title: Rose quartz : poems / Sasha taqwšeblu LaPointe.
Description: Minneapolis, Minnesota : Milkweed Editions, 2023. | In the author name, the 'w' is printed as a superscript and the 'e' is printed as a schwa in 'taqwšeblu'. | Summary: "A wild, seductive debut collection that presents a powerful journey of struggle and healing-and a spellbinding brew of folklore, movies, music, and ritual"-- Provided by publisher.
Identifiers: LCCN 2022029746 (print) | LCCN 2022029747 (ebook) | ISBN 9781571315434 (paperback) | ISBN 9781571317568 (ebook)
Subjects: LCGFT: Poetry.
Classification: LCC PS3612.A64394 R67 2023 (print) | LCC PS3612. A64394 (ebook) | DDC 811/.6--dc23/eng/20220628
LC record available at https://lccn.loc.gov/2022029746
LC ebook record available at https://lccn.loc.gov/2022029747

Milkweed Editions is committed to ecological stewardship. We strive to align our book production practices with this principle, and to reduce the impact of our operations in the environment. We are a member of the Green Press Initiative, a nonprofit coalition of publishers, manufacturers, and authors working to protect the world's endangered forests and conserve natural resources.

For the ones who carry wounds and for the healers who tend to them, for the seers and the conjurers, for the girls who scattered breadcrumbs but never found their way home, and invented one instead . . .

CONTENTS

III. ROSE QUARTZ / THE LOVERS

IV. MOONSTONE / THE HIGH PRIESTESS

"These are my ruby red lips
The better to suck you dry
These are my long red nails
The better to scratch out your eyes."
—"Lil' Red," by Bikini Kill

"I've got my own sword in my own hand
I've got my own plan that only I can know
Don't be sighing
Don't be crying
Your day will come
Your day alone
Years you'll know and a life you'll grow
Got a way to go all on your own."
—"It's My Way," by Buffy Sainte-Marie

"The first steps were a walk in the light
The next few tore the day from the night
And there needed to be waves but they grew so big in size
Scattered my body across the sky."
—"Sun," by Erica Freas

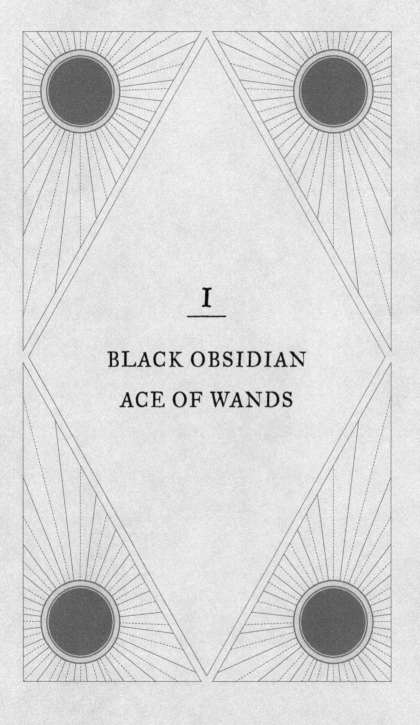

I

BLACK OBSIDIAN
ACE OF WANDS

Red Paint

all it ever was
                        a blanket
sagging off my shoulders
in the smoke
thick night
                        her hands
as they scooped it up
against the pounding
                        of drums
how they thundered
my limbs in storm-song
                        the four stars
I counted outside
the only window
like ghosts
                        the smoke as it escaped
leaving behind
its orange glow
                        and the dancers
                        cedar woven
my eyes falling heavy
past three in the morning
and this is when she tells me
                        the red paint
is for healing

Teach Me to Say I Love You

in your language
I have forgotten how to speak
something caught in my throat
a fish bone splintering me
into something quiet
muted and starlike
lost in a sky
the word for sky
was   šəqulgʷədxʷ

teach me to say
just stay   stay put   stay here
because I have forgotten
to be inside my own body

whatever my body has become
beneath your tongue
conquered and ugly
malformed and mispronounced

teach me a word
better than survivor
something more
like watching my grandmother
pour black coffee in the kitchen
and the stacks of legal pads
filled up with her words
I tried to hear

the word for language
was   gʷədgʷadad

teach me to say I love you
because every time I walk
into a restaurant to meet a date
I hesitate I remember
the trees along Portland Avenue

in their red bows
like gifts
on Christmas morning

this is to honor
assault survivors

how my mother tied each one
hugging their bark
in ribbon

and I think of this
as he pulls the chair out
takes my jacket
pours the wine red
into the glass
and asks
if I am hungry

red is what I remember
when I realize he will try
to take me home and have to learn
how to unwrap me

teach me to say I love you
because what good is a ribbon
if it cannot hold us together
where we have been broken

teach me to speak
in a language older than words
not of white men
whose tongues touch everything

quiet yourself and listen

ʔuʔušəbicid čəd

Ohh-ohh-sha-beet-see chud

like a sigh I would make
as a child comfortable and safe
then the thud of my heart
as it beats in my chest
its thrum as it drums
inside my rib cage

The Canoe My Grandmother Gave Me

*When my grandmother hit the record button on the cassette recorder, it startled
my great-aunt. What is it? What does it do? It's going to capture the language, my
grandmother said, to keep it. My great-aunt thought about this a long while. As a
child, she traveled by river, by inland waters to relatives, to bring them fish, to carry
the news. She looked down at the cassette recorder and nodded. Ah, she said. This
is just a different kind of canoe.*

The last time we ate together
we sat by a picture window
overlooking the channel
she pushed fried oysters
around her plate
chardonnay pooling
on white linen

at six I licked frosting
bone white from china
my mother embarrassed
reached for the plate
my grandmother slapped her hand away
just let her enjoy it
and we rotated high above the city
the Space Needle spinning clouds
into sugar

she looked over oysters
out past the docks remember
when all of this was underwater
she pointed a greasy fork

to the hill beyond the bridge
we kept the dead up there
before they came
and built a church

I see canoes high above a white chapel
in branches of trees
no longer there

speeding along
La Conner Whitney
the back seat sticky with whiskey
the smell of cow shit of cut grass
I look out at the snaking body
of water contained
curling and flexing to keep up

it was all underwater
she'd say until they came
and built dikes and farmhouses
planted fields just for tulips
stretching lakes of daffodils

with my head against glass
bottle in my lap
I squint until the channel breaks free
until the roads are water again

when I woke to find him there
breathing heavy blond
two hundred and ten pounds of quarterback
of animated Coors Light

above me
I learned to sever head from heart
dunked my head beneath water
that was no longer there
to drown again and again
to breathe in river silt and mud
count silver scales of fish
and all the white pebbles
rushing past

we learn to say
I just let it happen
we learn to use words
in forgotten languages
I learned to hold my breath
beneath the currents
unaware of the boat
on the riverbank
waiting there

Violet Rose

There was going to be a little girl

her name Violet   instead
a pitcher of milk spilling across
the kitchen floor a birth of stars
falling emptying the sky bringing
the cosmos straight into my living
room into my body filling my eyes
blinked me black and silver devoid
of life now I am celestial cold and
flickering planets forming from the
stardust in me ovarian cysts and
all the tiny stones that circle

Saturn orbiting empty

Obscurial and Other Spells for Survival

a mother and a girl a curl in the back
bent mountains of her knees
against the rushing of cedar
little fingers go from glass
to a wound beneath the belly
she is checking to see
if she is still intact
are the guts here the liver the stomach
the heart

or is she in pieces
a thing taken apart
she searches in the back of a Buick
for a lost thing
a firework turned inside out
blackening the car
in a cloud of gunpowder
and smoke

a shadow mass of soot needles
sends the car aspin
ditchward
throws the girl ten feet
from the crumpled metal
of what used to be
the backseat

it begins with an accident
a girl wakes on the forest floor
makes her way to the road
to find her mother
taking inventory of the wreckage
shaking her head over
an upside-down engine

but the look
on her mother's face
upon that charcoal black
amassing above her little girl
and gasping not realizing
she had taken
two steps
back

so the girl learns loneliness
and how to climb trees
escape the thing
that hewed like a storm
to her insides

weave cedar ropes
in the hopes of holding it in
bind the self to nurse logs
for whole moon cycles

but in the dark of a gymnasium
with a boy's hands clasped at her waist
she sways back and forth
to Boyz II Men

again

a fire that eats itself
back to blackness
blacks out the dance floor
the boy and the bathroom stall
she falls into puking tar in the toilet

when she thought to release it
neither scissors nor seam ripper
would sever it
if Peter Pan could somehow
escape his shadow why not her
but the darkness clung harder
she learned to like the taste of it
ate it every day back
into the bloodstream

on her wedding night
she snatched it trapped it up inside
a plastic bag and emptied it
into a bell jar
the mantel placed upon her
the new home

there they watched
the thing crawl and spin
caught within
glass walls
an apparition lost
without its host

it begins with dishes
with bags of peaches
from the fruit stand
paint samples and leaves raked
baked goods red velvet cakes

a hairline fracture
over time cracks
even the foundation

and when he came home
there was nothing left
save a small bit of fabric
from her dress

feathering
into ash

Blue

I emerge from our yellow linoleum bathroom blue
at one end of our single-wide trailer
and I have the length of narrow hallway to consider
before reaching the living room blue
Blue!? And I know my mother is furious
You look ridiculous it's all she says
and I do I had torn the pages from a magazine
lined my bedroom floor with them and studied
those punk rock spiked hair white teeth
high fashion popped collar leather studded glossy photos
strewn across my small space like a spread of tarot cards
telling me a future I would never get to
not out here *not* in the white trailer rusting amber
thick of trees stretch of reservation of highway
that stood between me and whatever else was out there
record stores the mall parking lots where kids were skateboarding
and smoking pot probably kids with boom boxes and bottles of beer
out there were beaches with bands playing on them
and these faces these shining faces with pink green purple and blue hair
blue I *could* get *that* at least
I could mix seventeen packets of blue raspberry Kool-Aid
with a little water and I could get *that*
it was alchemy it was potion making
but no one told me about the bleach
about my dark hair needing to lift
to lighten in order to get that blue
no one told me that the mess of Kool-Aid
would only run down my scalp my face my neck
would stain me blue

Blue is what you taste like
he says still holding me on the twin bed
in the glow of dawn my teenage curiosity
has pushed me to ask *What does my body taste like to you*
his fingers travel from neck to navel
breath on my thigh and here in our sacred space
he answers simply *Blue you taste blue*
and I wonder if what he means is sad
you taste sad

taqʷšəblu
the name is given to me
when I am three
to understand it
my child brain has to break it apart
taqʷšəblu
talk as in talking
as in to tell as in story
sha as in the second syllable
of my English name
as in half of me
blue as in the taste of me
blue as in sad

my grandmother was taqʷšəblu
before me and now I am
taqʷšəblu too

Hansel and Gretel

Rocking back and forth by the boom box, hugged knees to my chest all sugar and sweat. Aluminum can't keep me here, not when there's a window that leads to the woods that leads to the highway. My way to escape. Headphones, backpack, stolen quarters from a jar. I walk Indian Road toward the water. Dip a toe into the channel. Imagine freezing. Lungs crushed against the weight of blue. The overpour. The indigo night. The golden glow of headlights as they fight toward me. Send the blue shattered glass back to shadow. Climb into the cab of a stranger's truck. *Anywhere but here.*

And you told me

be back before nightfall

be back before they call your name

but you had to have known as you stood alone

against our trailer

to bring your sister in for dinner

a game of pretend or was it something else?

as you called out again

again to no one

Pony

I carried a jar big and fragile
glass in my hands
asking strangers
for money

along the Nooksack
I was barefoot I was ten
I was saving to buy a pony

because the salmonberries
weren't good enough
the wool blankets weren't
good enough

for me to be a real
Indian
like the ones in the movies
I was going to need
to buy a pony

and paint it
ride off into war on it
or become part of it like
The Girl Who Loved Wild Horses
or whatever

I wasn't sure
what I would do with it
just that it wasn't
a canoe

or a longhouse

it was something
living something

Indian

Little Red

Highway-side and thumb out swaying against cow manure. That is how it started. I found a jar of dye to cover the blue. Pillar Box, Fire Engine, Vampire, and Blood. Painted delicately over the bruise. Russian Red lipstick like a gash across my face. Laced up my combat boots, pulled a hood of fur snow-white against the sky to shield me. And I took to walking. Past farmhouse, past station, past old barn burned and dilapidated. My breath my only company, my hair waving like a small fire on the valley. A call alarming: Find me.

Find me.

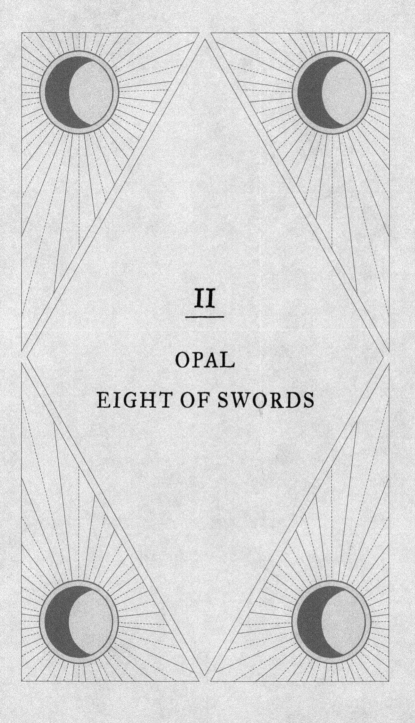

II

OPAL

EIGHT OF SWORDS

Black Salt

Draw me encircled

in something other

than gasoline. I am
tired of burning—

black salt, circle me
from striking sparks

against the dark but
come swallowing

that shadow

I tried to pretend

wasn't part of me.

Beekeeper

You heard the buzzing of a hundred
wings first

a slow machine of fluttering
you listened at the top

of the spiral stair
that led you there

you opened to a shadowed
space alive with candlelight

and insects crawling
the walls

the honeycombed tower of
her sweet tomb

a thousand bees between
you and her body

honeysuckle fireweed
that stinging itch

the burn you learn to ignore
because your tongue tastes

of honey

The Black Lodge

I should not have tried to follow her down, to follow the lure of
breadcrumbs. But one by one I touched them to my fingertips and
ate them. I wore a vial of poison around my neck and held death
for safekeeping. And there was nobody. No Special Agent Dale
Cooper, no Audrey, no Log Lady to call my bluff. All I've ever
wanted was safety, cherry pie, the consistency of coffee, black.

Time Turner

You knew precisely what to do
the copper face of time around your neck

how many clicks will it take to
reach her

teenaged and tangled with a boy
in braces at the skate shop

this isn't the place
her face has already gone

quiet turn back further
find her wielding a razor

ruby drops of blood
studding a beige carpet

keep clicking 16 through 15 pass Jack
Daniel's pass Mad Dog 20/20

pass bonfires pass mushroomed evenings as
she a shivering thing

clung to the base of a cedar pearls of
vomit strand from her lips

consider stopping here to brush
away the hair and sweat

and keep going

skip over 14 can't risk running
into yourself

and then it happens

you love her even then though you are
grown and she is 10

several limbs up a tree she sucks berries
from sap-stuck fingers

coax her down her eyes bright moons
her hair wild this child still

and her hand curled around your
hand small and untouched

the skin on her thighs scraped
only by bark

encircle her in a length of
golden chain

whisper her name

and speak

Little Red: Against Me

Rain-soaked and weary, over mountains, over roads. I am looking for something other than the glow of headlights, beyond the river, beyond the mall. Something bigger than the blue night. A fight against the cold. I crest the hill into free fall. Trees shape-shift into buildings. The river has always been a highway, cans of beer like fish, silver in my bag. I can last out here. The men in cars have changed into wolves. I disappear down the side streets to shake them. Run fast over branches and bent trees, and a basement's noisy door opens to me.

Hands wrapped in bracelets. Fingers sweaty and curled into fists. I never knew a sound could have a color. A blistering heat. Lamp lit like firelight. Shadows slammed and danced along concrete. Below earth I fell into bodies. Had to find my footing as the red reached out to me its screaming.

Filled me up from the inside. Ignited the pool in me like a match to gasoline. And I shouted as the people tumbled their limbs like lovers against me.

Devil's Night: The Central District

I asked Kurt Cobain for directions
as he stoop-sat skull blown open like
a tin can
he handed me an invitation

cut and pasted his face wrecked
I stepped over the body parts of gutted beasts
entrails and blood pumping hearts
adorned the front room like party favors

Elizabeth Báthory served up a glass deep
red and bubbling from a punch bowl
I pull out my own flask
always trust your own whiskey at a party
and make my way to the dance floor

where cannibals eat each other
like flank steaks they grind and sway
devouring fingers toes and legs a sickening
display caught in the neon-lit fog

werewolves chase ghost girls in the dark
not even the apparitions recognize me
in their leather jackets as they ask
who are you supposed to be

I hold up my shackled hands crushed
beneath the thumb screws my hair piled high
in ringlets and this dress

a blood-spattered Viking yells at me *you must be*
a princess his voice crushed in my ear
his weight and meat and muscle against my entire
body yellow hair falling

too close to my head he threatens
to violate me right here
in front of the brain-hungry dead
but I am not a princess and that woman my
finger points to a burned and breastplated
Joan of Arc is my handmaiden and together

we will sever your head
from your body
and you will feel cold metal
I pull the sword from my skirt with my iron
knuckles shining because this is the ring

you gave me

and these are your promises

What He Should Have Had

It's not fair says my
brother talking at me over
his pint glass

I belong on a yacht we
had that you know we
had a yacht

we never had a yacht
you mean one of mom's boyfriends did I poke
at the red-filmed ice of my spent Bloody Mary
I order another as my brother continues his story
of what we should have had

all that shit he
says *those rich*
guys those condos
in the city

but she moved us to
Swinomish

at this there is a long sigh an
eye roll another beer in his
fist and he drinks it angrily

and I am noticing
how handsome my
brother is

his pitch-colored hair his jaw
his big smile how he looks
like Superman like Freddie
Prinze Jr. in some romantic
comedy made for teenagers
in the nineties

driving back up the coast to
our ancestral home I sleep in
the woods send him pictures of
whales and a roadside motel
we stayed in as kids

but he is busy with his
list of all the things we
should have had

he is writing them down
and marking them off

when we say goodbye I
watch my older brother try
not to cry

I tell him to be less
angry

but it's too late my brother has
already pulled out his boning
knife

look what happened to you

he repeats it

he carves a fish-shaped hole
right into me

look what happened to you

Little Red: Potion Making

Take this on your tongue and swallow. Little. Round. Red. A wolf's head imprinted, its jaws within. We tumble into coat check, a thrill of lips met and kissed amidst other people's jackets. And I woke beneath a pile of coats. Parted denim and leather to glimpse into a world beyond lions & witches & wardrobes, where for hours I was a queen thronged in victory, not battle. Not heavy with the ache of many wounds but loosed into dancing. Guitars so loud it seemed the whole place had overcome something. The beer spills from plastic chalices, and the mess may remain. We don't need to pick it up. It was never ours to begin with.

Half Moon Bay

Half Indian
an old woman laughs
I must take after
a white father
because I can   *pass*

they say the tribes
lived along the coast
all along San Francisco Bay

driving alongside waves
I feel alone
feel home drift away

the moon hooks the sky
and I drive trying to catch it
between my fingers
a crescent of white
a fight still present

Garbage Indians
the old woman told me
that's what we called them
growing up in Monterey

the dump was on their reservation
because isn't it always
and I bite my tongue until it bleeds
until I quiet the anger in me

and I'll wait until I leave
Half Moon Bay
to scream into my fist
and say all the things
we are not supposed to say

to the people who are older than us

Rose Gold

untethered I locate the sea
and step into it

I want to be held by something
saltwater and weeds

wrapping around me
the sting of a fresh cut

the sun burns off
layer by layer

first my clothing
then my skin

delicate papyrus
shaking off

reptilian sarcophagus
opening

a faint glow
below wounds

hieroglyphs inked
in gold

Monarch

I watched a Hawaiian monarch
float the salt air of a wave
like its small form was somehow
meant to do this
pulled down
catapulted forward
launched up again and again
into the spray

unable to look away
I began to worry after all
it was only a matter of time
before this little thing
paper thin and fragile
would be swallowed

persimmon-colored wings
and bold black
splattered against volcanic rock
in a brocade of lace
and tissue

of course this never happens
but that doesn't stop me
from imagining
wings blown apart
and spread

like a mounted specimen
upon the beach
a flag of warning

that none of the others
will see

Breadcrumbs

I opened a pocketknife
to my ankle and cut
open the skin
I was looking for something
that red I had heard about that shade
I was told would heal me

I opened to a lover
who couldn't find it either
instead got lost in the pink folds of me
never scarlet never crimson or ruby
a red maybe
but not in that blood way

away my brother
went looking for it too
like Hansel and Gretel
lost in those woods
there is a memory
of us in pajamas
though it is afternoon
and we are eating cereal
off the floor like animals

but brother you slowly
crawled up the walls
through the doorway
and ate every green yellow and blue
Froot Loop before me

our mother I thought Sleeping Beauty
but you knew better
something about gingerbread and sweets
a fear so real you crawled out
leaving the glow of the static ghosts
dancing on the TV

June ninth I make a cake carve into its
white skin cut open to red velvet and it's
never as red as I want it to be

I light candles

blow them out
I light them again

I do this until I am ready
to eat the whole thing

in one sitting

The Queen's Bath

I don't want to go
to sugar plantations
or museums

like other people's
money the word
plantation

makes me uneasy
and the word vacation
a fish swallowing another fish

walking along wet
concrete

I stop to talk
to a man selling
shave ice

remember

the word
makes me
angry

I don't want to see
the missionaries
carved bed frames
Bible tables
or Pearl Harbor posters

I want to see   this
roaring ocean
volcanic rock

ringing a pool

of blue the sign

that reads
many people
have drowned here

this joy that swells in me
like the surf coming in
might take me
out to sea
and of course I wonder

what kind of queen
was she

Rose Hips

lick the skin along my
outer thigh

hip bone and curved
waist

we levitate tangled
in rafters

above a stage somewhere
in Sweden

your fingers travel
neck to navel

like the tour we're on
you explore the map

of my body

had I known this
would one day

take you away
from me

I would have drawn it out a little
longer

the sun comes up
over Gothenburg

an American girl
on her way to Morocco

fills my fist with
rose hips

for the hangover

Sparkwood and 21

In the black lodge of my living room, red tick of alarm clock pulsing, Laura Palmer strikes like a match, setting fire to everything. Beneath a netting of medication, a sort of healing. It begins on the sofa. That's how I know she's here to show me something about myself. Out in those woods she's been waiting. Beneath branches. Standing below the amber glow of owl eyes, breaking pitch with embers' slow ignition. This is where I get to know her. A spark in the rain-swept city. She curls her finger in my hair to make sure I'm listening. Now comes her breath on kindling. A whispered story *fire walk with me* my body, a curled leaf alone on the pullout. Pill-spelled in the witching hour. In the dark between worlds, it is not a coincidence the two of us met here, where a girl's story can fall across an entire town, like pine needles.

The Black Gates

A hobbit jade in my window
is spiraling brown along its edges
I've never learned
to take care of anything
smaller than myself

beyond the window
a grown man in dirty clothes
walks along the darkening
Duwamish

polluted waters
dead marshes

there was once a great
battle here among men

this man crushes a can
of 211 throws it into my yard
makes his way to the edge of the water
and opens another

for his fallen comrades

Newlywed

I wanted to make you a blueberry pie
this afternoon all sugar and rolling pins
all fingerprints and flour I've heard that's
what wives do

instead I stared at the ceiling
began to worry what you would do
with me come five o'clock and you open the door
throw down your keys and find me

in a forest of cardboard and wrapping
a mess of discarded wedding gifts because
I don't actually know what to do
with a Le Creuset

and maybe I haven't even made it
to the kitchen or the piecrust maybe
I've smashed all the berries
between my fingers

one by one

and you'll find me
in the wilderness
of our living room
crawling on my hands
and knees juicy blue war paint
across my cheeks

and you'll clean me up like you do
draw a bath check for sharp objects
broken glass and you'll leave the door cracked
as you play guitar in the next room

but what if it isn't enough this time
when I climb from the deep well of that tub
crawl into bed still warm and slippery
and you touch me
and I know you want me

to be better

will you drive me to the edge
of the city at sundown

will you touch my neck
the whole way
will you tell me it's better
this way

as you leave me
at the line of trees

shadow branches
reaching out like hands

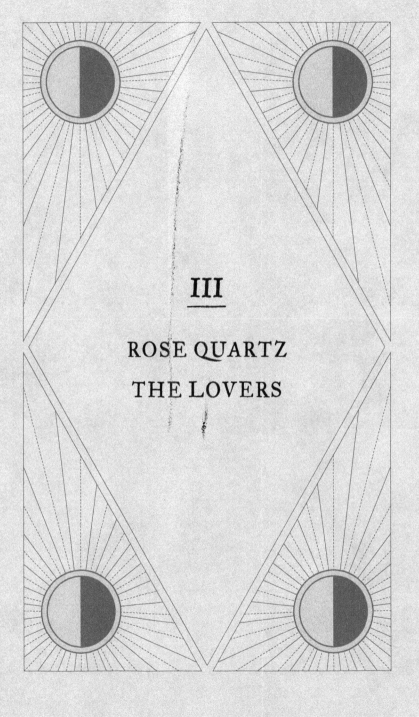

III

ROSE QUARTZ
THE LOVERS

The White Lodge

I dug a moonstone from the wet earth and swallowed it. Tired of my convalescence. I drank it down with the mud and insects, small pebbles: debris against my teeth. I climbed the tallest tree. Edged out across its branches. Removed my dress. Cut my hair. Watched it float down. Raven black like falling feathers. And I didn't jump. I didn't need to. Nor did I wait to be rescued—a great horned owl, snow-white, perched beside me, saying nothing.

The Queen's Bath

The moon hangs
its sliver of shaved light

as above
so below

weightless for now
circled in salt and reef

swelling
I ask for protection

as the water changes
from indigo to orange

like fire
as the sun sinks

as the red fades to meet me

where sapphire and rose
collide

becoming   Violet

Rose Quartz

A Coney Island witch her tent in the shadow
of the decaying Wonder Wheel
put her fingers to my chest

sugar spun pink and popcorn
the photo booth that held the ghosts
of Robert and Patti
the whir of a wooden roller coaster
mechanical phantoms
the haunted house
all witnesses
to her prediction:

your heart is broken

she turned to a wall of jars
all glittering with stones
with her prophecy she tried to sell me
a rock pink and ugly
I told her she was wrong
she held the rock to my heart

*if it's not now
then it will be*

like a curse her stone followed me
back to the West Coast showed
up dangling next to a shark tooth
an earring my friend says or
holding it to my chest *a necklace*

another gift a crystal wand
a pendant all the way
from London

I know you don't like pink
my friend says to me
but I thought of you anyway

rose perfume rose tea rose cakes
and wine all came to me
I put them in shoeboxes
I put them under the bed
hid them all over the house
but at night they came
thorns around my chest
and I forgot how to breathe
my husband sleeping next to me
could not reach me
through the bramble

so I took to walking at night
in the neighbor's gardens
fragrant roses plucked one by one
dropped them
to the ground
like a bonfire of spinning wheels
it was preventative

but the thorns climbed up
the gutters and into the windows and when my husband
asked me to stay

I called him selfish
beat my fists against
his chest because
he had already turned
into a pale pink ice

one by one the things
in the house turned to stone
I lost records and jackets
pots and pans two cats and even a dog
hardened into blush crystal

the television the furniture
and the house now empty
wrapped in my wedding blanket
and laughing the witch had won
hadn't she

when I moved into the new house
I wouldn't open the boxes marked "Coney Island"
entombed inside all those roses

stashed beneath my bed
their annoying pink glow
kept me up at night
until one morning
I gave birth
to a   rosebud
still   unmoving
deep   deep   red

and that's when I felt it
the breaking of
crystal splinters
of glass smashed
along the concrete

my skin
was leaving
my body

organs hardening

I tore the box open
to the pink light
bathed in rose oil
drank down the rose wine
ate petals
swallowed thorns

and covered myself

womb to sternum
in stones

Rose Red

I woke in the glass coffin of my bedroom. I watched the color go: first the fingertips, then the white traveling up my arm's length. Both legs, thighs. The rib cage and neck. Lips the color of blood drained slow. Bone lit. No glow of rose-tinted cheeks. I experimented with rouge, dyes, and paint. I covered myself in rubies, but beneath the glimmer was skin as white as snow. Ice-cold. Frozen over. This medication, they said, keep taking it. For the pain.

Rose Oil

I will build the fire up from the scrap wood
of a wrecked home tending it as other women
do their children on starless nights

I will drop my gown at the crackling embers
see my silhouette against flame and raise
each finger to the sky in want
in wailing

limbs painted in rose oil and clay
I will lose my name in the billowing smoke
will sing a circle inside salt lines

to forget the words of earth
and levitate

Snow-White

The taste on tongue metallic. How everything frosted over looks like heaven. Disappointing and sterile. Take one. This glass of water. Take two. Watch the throat grow alabaster, pearl. You have sutured the wounds. Yet still feel the need for red. Spread it out along the bedsheets. You need to feel something. So you tiptoe down the hall and buy all the licorice rope from a vending machine. Red wine spills from a plastic bag like someone else's IV kicked over. Red roses from the gift shop. Red Hots and Hot Tamales torn from their boxes and scattered all over the counter. Your offering: a bottle of nail polish swiped from the nurse's lounge, a grandfather's handkerchief, and two squares of red velvet cake, the frosting licked off, 'cause isn't there already enough white in this room? Your plastic cup of Jell-O. One wilted strawberry, a teddy bear gripping a heart in its paws that reads GET BETTER SOON. The fire extinguisher gleams in the center of your altar: a gathered beacon, its red light shines across these banks of snow.

In the Belly of the Wolf

Deep red, crimson walls pulsate with breath, and a booming heartbeat surrounds me. I can crawl up along the tongue, but a prison of teeth pushes me back down. Over and over I fall into a pool of blood and bones. I let myself sink to the bottom. Float down into the muck. I am waiting, but for what? There is no huntsman. No one to gun down the wolf and fetch me from its belly. When I hear its pulse pounding, I splash upward. *This beast will go on living.* Each beat of its heart tells me, *It will survive and I will not.* The beating gets louder, faster. The red walls vibrate with each thunder, like drums, like dancing. I will not sink to the bottom. Instead I dig far down in the belly, to the many bones. I find a curved rib bone and scrape it along the rough tongue, sharpening, so sharp it only takes one deep thrust and I pierce that animal's flesh. I cut open all the way through the skeleton, the meat, and the muscle. I woke in the belly of a beast. I pull myself out through its matted fur and take one full breath in the daylight.

Mount Saint Helens

The woman to my right reads *The Bell Jar*
the man to my left is tattooed *Ulysses*
the teal surface of the water
holds Seattle's August green beneath

like it, I want to be held by something
like seagrass as it wraps around my knees
I fight the urge to spring upward
to find silence to find space without words
find my lungs filling with water

breaking the surface
of Lake Washington
its books and beers are still here
the dock littered with limbs
and mouths open

Mount Rainier to the right
I look north to Baker
I float between two mountains
and remember the legend

Saint Helens
my grandmother told
of a love story
so old
it was ancient

Rainier and Baker fought
over her

and when she couldn't take their tug of
war her head exploded

flooding the valley
with fire

climbing the ladder
I drip water onto a stranger
lie back out as a woman sighs
and turns a page the man with the tattoo
is talking loudly about South America
and volcanoes
my skin warms beneath the sun
I plunge down into the deep
again a rescue helicopter

as it drops its water
I am trying to put out the flames

I dive in climb back
rush the surface
sink back float up

here I levitate

the mountains left to mourn
face each other every day

the sun blazes behind
the rippling me
reflected and shining

the rays of light bursting
out the late afternoon like
fire catching have

crowned me

Portland Rose Garden

Just leave it he said pulling me
through the hedges

I walked with the sun
through the rose garden

my dress caught the thorns
again and again until it fell shredded

with his tongue he pushed a petal into
my mouth told me to swallow

I began to eat them by the fistful
Amalia, Imperial, and Eternity

Beach Rose and Sunsprite but when I came
to the Poet's Wife

I lost my appetite
wife in my fingertips

unable to devour it
as the sun began to set

I plucked from his head one
golden hair threaded a hundred scarlet

petals into a blanket
because I wanted to stay here

I pulled the roses over my body
to sleep in fragrant dark

Your Nights

if we are going to be together
we are going

to need a system
of rules a treaty

an understanding you won't
colonize my body but you'll

come when you're invited
bring gifts to the borders of me

we'll learn to say thank you
in each other's languages

we'll learn the important phrases
don't stop and *I love you*

we're going to need to reach
some kind of agreement

your nights versus *my nights*

my nights are all leather and fatherless
dark all chasing pain and holding it there

your nights are for words and
holding things that are fragile

my nights are a cat of nine tails
against skin are all the things that
come

bubbling and beading to the surface
your nights are *remember when we were young*

my nights are Japanese rope bondage
your nights are watercolors and cherry blossoms

I asked you to cover my mouth with your
hand I was feeling adventurous and after all

it was my night darling you refused
you couldn't stand to see me silenced

Rose Moon

Lit rose the smoke
curled along my
breast like a tongue

I have taken the sun
for a lover a foolish
thing since I have
always been the
moon

pale and shadowed
uncertain how it is
tide ever crawls to
shore

under my guidance my
wax and waning my
unchanging dark

the sun is a bright bright
blinding fire swollen and
radiant

this dance this unsustainable
spark

Fox Hunt

I'd scare you
it's the first thing
you say to me

poolside and hiding
behind sunglasses
a grin that bares teeth

like California
pavement
before rain
like you could
smell something
on me

my date offers
his hand
holds my beer
as we crawl
through the window
of the two-story hotel

out on the roof
I recite Jawbreaker lyrics
in the midnight heat
looking in our lamplit room
still thinking about teeth

I am thinking about your jaws
what might be carried in them
what might be a carcass in them

devoured and taken
back to all the things
you have already eaten

we wander the hallways
you disappear
up a stairway
your silhouette
moves like smoke

you're a specter
in a nice shirt
full of tequila
an apparition
haunting the lobby

with a pretty blonde
on your arm
like a trophy
or a pelt

still I'm interested
curious and longing
for interruption
because even as a child
I always loved
a villain

my date plays Pac-Man
and we touch a piano
that we aren't supposed to
we ask the receptionist
for a corkscrew she just nods
and points us
to the Red Fox Room

in my dreams we're taxidermied
all hair and bone
animals open and frozen
locked in wanting
memory is funny
like that

and I see you
beneath neon
ghostlike and alone
under the shadows
of mouths

like a chase
that has ended
like hunting parties
gone home

and your booth is dark
and your face is tired
and soon we will return
to our rooms
to our dates

stiff white sheets

traps sprung

and empty

S.O.T.D.

mixtapes are the new
smoke signals
this distance traversed
by Joy Division
by Sonic Youth
by all the things
you found
in the post-punk
section

send me song lyrics
send me passages
send me anything
you made that day
and stay with me
a moment longer

brush strokes
and skate videos
did you know
Henry Miller
sent Anaïs Nin
love letters

two friends
entangled
in language

remember when
we went to Paris
remember the bridge
and the wine
we've never been to Paris
but if your memory
is as bad as mine
there is no one
to blow our cover

so let us dance awhile
and the miles between us are
only part of the choreography

are you still awake
are you still at the party

maybe one day
we'll marry

other people
and we won't be
at the other's
wedding

but we'll raise a glass
and ask
have you heard this one

another song
that reminds me of you

Slouching Towards Bethlehem
and *Perfume*

a photograph
a cup of coffee
the stranger
at the show

you should know
that I'm always
thinking

about

you

Rosewood

I grind belladonna
opium poppies
and datura

the skin of a toad and
seven rosebuds into
a red paste

taste my lover on my
tongue again and open
the sky

riding the black
air the space
between

my thighs is alive
with stars and
moonlight

flying ointment
slick wood

and the whole world
passes beneath me

I float over you
looking in

you never even
knew

I was coming

The Lost Boys

Drink this and be one of us
my brother passed
his bottle of wine to me
tried to offer life eternal
he was always trying to fix things

but this highway is haunted
the coast and its ghosts remind me
that I am broken

my brother has become
something immortal
and he didn't even
have to die first
his thirst
for a better life
turned him
into darkness

and my mother tried to grieve
but it is hard to mourn
the living

so I tell her he is dead
because gone is better than missing
gone is a ghost you can blow out
the candle for

it is my duty to take him apart
to burn the letters rip down the flyers
drive the stake through his heart

because you cannot hang posters
for lost children pretending
they will one day come home
because at some point you realize
the pictures were for you

so for her I have become
a vampire hunter
armed with garlic
and holy water
but the truth is
I can't do it
the truth is
behind fangs I still see
the lost boy
who used to be
my brother

so when he offered the wine
that was his blood
I took a swallow
tried to follow him
in shadow

but I remembered my promise
not to become a daughter missing
had to quit the ritual halfway

and watch my brother
say hello to the night
and fight alone

in Santa Cruz
I cry into my beloved's hands
and abandon immortality
and he knows how hard this is for me
knows my capacity
for vanishing

so I anchor myself to him
and watch the waves
return to shore
I whisper a spell
of protection
for my brother

for all the lost boys
who came before

Little Red: Teeth

Awake a fairy ring. *Amanita muscaria.* And dancing. A record player still spins somewhere beyond the wood. Needle against nothing. And my eyelashes brush against jawbone: matted fur, teeth lined up, bone pearls around my neck, and dripping crimson. Blood dressed. Ruby gown down to my ankles. And I pick myself up. Toes naked in the mud and moss as I cross the grove to find you. Kneel at your feet. Present to you its steaming pelt. But you do not recognize me.

All you could ever see was teeth.

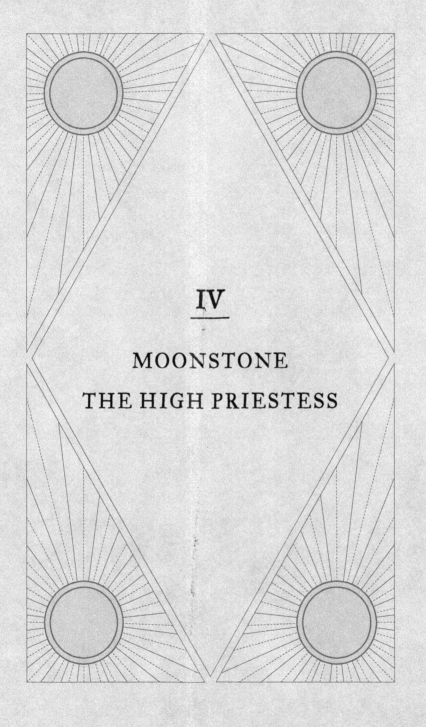

IV

MOONSTONE
THE HIGH PRIESTESS

Gretel: Song

I sat alone in a diamond. Followed bread crumbs back to a rain-soaked pitcher's mound. A diamond without. A diamond missing something. Not even a dugout. Just a bit of plywood and chain link. Here, we lived as children. Across the lot a stand of trees. Beyond the pines smoke rising from chimneys. In front of all of this sits the longhouse. Wet, empty. Two hundred feet of wood stand quietly. Inside I build a fire. I start dancing. And I sing to the charred pillars. Black bones reach upward to the ceiling.

Are you here now?

Are you here now?

Were you ever even coming?

Primrose and Wolverine

if I wake up tomorrow
I will float primrose
down the river
and watch it disappear

yesterday this desire
to see it gone
I sheared my hair

and when the cut flowers
showed up on the nightstand
I asked why
you said just because
and I should have known better
it's never just because

you don't believe
the warning
yet you took me
to the movies
tried to hide me
from whatever it was
that was coming

Cherry Coke in the dark
and this Wolverine
a violent and wild thing
thrashing the movie screen
applause and laughter

how fast this father is
to protect this vicious darling
this brown-haired girl fighting

survival is a funny thing
when it is choreographed
I grabbed my belly as I felt it
tripped over the red chair

went running through the parking lot
popcorn falling behind me
all along the wet pavement
like buttered snow
shoppers hurried past
open-mouthed as you
fought to get me
inside the car

because when I knew
what was happening
when I showed you

my fingers
dripping
in red

I let my mouth
I let my throat
I let my limbs

I never felt more like an animal

Lifting the Sky

in the distance
the clouds begin to fall
gray rain too far to matter

oceanward it has gone dark
everywhere but here
circle of campfire
crackling orange

against a roar of waves
against that rain
against world's end
an island sits quiet
keeps the dead in its trees

Elder Island
said a man on the beach
camera around his neck boy at his knees
poking starfish
said you can kayak around it
get real close to its shores

I turn away pull up
the hood of my sweatshirt
cover my face

now the sky is black
the waves only exist
because we can hear them
beyond the driftwood

my grandmother tells
how the people worked together
and I know the story
could recite it from memory
but I like the sounds
of Lushootseed
of English

I do not interrupt
I do not stop her I do not say
Grandmother

I've heard this one
I know how it ends
I finish the last bit of whiskey
from the metal mug
drop it to the sand and I hear
the click of cassette tape

the two speakers
that carry her voice
go to static
as I rewind and press play
one more time
and though it's quiet
they're always out there
with that big pole
saying *all together now*

as they get the sky
up where it belongs
and lift the world
out of darkness

again

Little Red: The Beginning

She woke to find she could not open her eyes. The eyelids twitched and strained, glued together and sticky. Pink dust blinked from their corners. Her mouth, she realized, was also stuck. She lifted a finger, dug open her lips. A deep red clay was caked over her face. She pulled the white sheets and the wool blankets back. Her small feet on the cabin floor. The woodstove in the middle of the room still exhaling warmth. Bits of fish left on the plate next to her grandmother's coffee mug. She looked to the old woman's cot across from hers. And then to the sink, then to the window, and finally to her grandmother's rocking chair as it fell: Forward. And back again.

This Riverbank

we gather in gray sand
to stand together

against fog-shrouded mountains
of pine

the rain raised the river
to dangerous heights

and even I am worried I
might drown here

they say it drops off swift
and takes swimmers

my friends wade out
like worried mothers

who stay close and yell
don't go beyond these
branches

they are trying to be
responsible a branch
won't keep me from
dying

and one tells me she wishes
she had rope

and even though she knows there is
none she is looking anyway

they want to hold on to
something but I am
already smoke knee-
deep in freezing water

I float six blue
candles down
the current and
scream

because none of this matters

I float white linen
and cedar

the river has reached my
rib cage and I curse not
the cold but because
you're not in there

and I feel you like
a missing tooth

I float vitamins and
rose petals a deck of
tarot cards whose good
fortune swirls the eddy

a piece of cake and your
picture the cold rush of
water against my chin

and I let myself fall in
with you

beneath the surface I
remember you in the palm
of my hand small and
ruined

nobody warned me about
the details of your toes and
fingers the violet berry of
your unformed eye

how perfect you were in
stillness

I see the water rushing
the bottom of a cup
chasing two pills down
after your father took
you from me put you in
the freezer so I could
sleep

take these he said and I
dreamt four days waking
some afternoons forgetting
everything

and now my friends are on the
riverbank shouting my English
name it hits the air and
evaporates against the trees it
turns into nothing
they cannot see the fingers
in my hair hands at my wrists
and feet holding gently my
given-up body

unwilling to let it go
breathless

with the others
down the Skagit
and I know why

this mountain
this valley this
riverbank

Half Moon Bay II

Here on the coast
things go missing
earthquakes
shake the shores
into the sea
and the colonizers
who buried languages
of conquered people
are vanishing

beyond the break
two whales breach
they rise and dip
like they're dancing

I fall in love with distance
the crashing waves
that will outlast us

tell me the bones
buried on the beach
will rise to the surface
like blood beading

tell me we are the whales midbreach
tell me all the things
we'll never touch
but aren't out of reach

In the Poison Garden

You said of my family we
were cursed specifically the
women sick

unable to be in my body I
got in the bath instead
blood red

with herbs and medicines I am
trying to fix it I am trying to wash
off the sickness

you said of my ancestry
affliction you said broken

like our wedding night I am trying to fight it I
am drowning in this need to fix it

to make myself more white not
just pale but *Lilium* that delicate
shade of maiden

less red you said it was my
mother and grandmother's
doing

said it was them who made the men in my
family death hungry it's true you knew the
stories

my grandfather how he wandered
the wood at sunset seeking ghosts
a generation later

my father wanders Tacoma
reaches the hospital pleading to
them *I'm dying*

of my wife's broken heart
that sad part of her that is
killing me

of the women I come from you said damaged
said historically said intergenerationally

from the red bathwater I am
remembering raccoons their small
paws curled into fists

how my mother must have seen
but didn't miss didn't hit the brakes

didn't even try to instead my
brothers heard the thuds

beneath tires as my mother
said nothing but continued
driving

you said of my family we were sick
specifically the women suffered
something

unnameable quiet
sickness opiate
numb

my mother was only trying to dull the
pain that had been gifted to her by
blood red

I am less white beneath my skin
unforgiven by you fooled into thinking I
was something else

of my face your mother said *didn't
look Indian* what then where do I
keep it if not on the skin

slice me open like a persimmon
watch blood pour out

in red ribbons
here is where I keep seeds in
my DNA you'll find a
catalogue a bouquet
of heirlooms coursing
written inside my body a
history

drink me and see the morning
my grandmother walked into the
sea

drink and see me below a stranger
and thrashing see red party cups
ringing my head in halo

see me bent over
white powder and
smiling

fistful of pills metallic on my tongue and
see how I turn off like clockwork

this numb is what we
gather now what we hold
in our baskets how

we keep coming back for it
like canned fish thimbleberries and
hops picked in summer

of the women of my family you
said addiction said submission

from the red bath I wrap
a towel around my
nakedness

bergamot and rose petal still
clinging to my breasts set the
cedar down carefully

and step to the mirror
to the face as it says shape
shift says shake this
off or wilt a pale
tulip tossed at his
feet

Redwoods

I told myself I'd never write
a poem about the redwoods
because it's been done
because I've made this trip
twice now with people
I have loved

and what's left to say
about old wood

I told you I'd be okay
as I left you curbside
in San Francisco drove away
to a sad nineties playlist
not crying along to the music
but in my best riot grrrl
kind of way

at least I had to make a fire
after a five-hour
drive had to watch
my sad vegan hot dogs
as they blistered
into something unnatural
in the flames

I am tired of writing
about old things
like grandmothers

and languages
that are dying
and these trees
big and mythic
too old to give a shit
about what is happening
in the cities
bodies gunned
down in the street
pandemics
police brutality
this old growth
just towering
like *we told you so*
like *you didn't see*
this coming

further north
and further from you
I swim in rivers and lakes
outside of Arcata
I already miss California
hot sand and sex and your face
when it is still sleeping

through Newport through Brookings
I am drumming my fingers
on the steering wheel
singing along
with Janet and Bikini Kill

if I was your girl
oh the things I'd do to you

pull off in a town that smells
of cow shit and seagrass
ignore the Trump signs
forget that I'm not allowed
to pump my own gas

make you call out my name
I'd ask who it belongs to

you asked me
to move in with you
and that's big
like Haystack Rock
like drive-in
movie theaters
their parking
lots all painted
and abandoned

and I am considering this
because I miss San Diego
miss your blond hair
warm pavement
and Bomb Pops
melting over my fingers
blue and sticky
like when I was a kid

how is it I have never dated
someone who is also Coast Salish
or at least Indigenous
instead it's Disney's Pocahontas

her animated dad with his hands up
these white men are dangerous
and I come running

maybe it's time I slept with someone
who understands me traditionally
who shares my spirit dreams
but you have your van
and that California tan
and you have kickflips and ollies
and I am a sucker for you
when you come home
from surfing
limping
because
of a stingray

today I am in Astoria
and the trees are different
here the sea is cold and gray
like it's supposed to be
and they say where you're from
never leaves your body
this land is in my blood
and it likes to remind me
you think I forgot
motherfucker
you redwoods
are a rude
awakening

I pass the places
that mark me Indian
the signs that point me
to the reservation
Deadman's Cove
and the Pioneer Museum
trailer homes like bones and seals
you can feed like dogs

you want me
to move in with you
and I am looking
at the succulents
on the dash
plucked from your yard
and jammed
into a makeshift planter
that once housed
LaCroix cans
wilted and thirsty for sun
a sweet memento
but I hate
how we've
displaced them

I am in love
with a white boy
from California
an artist a skateboarder
a beautiful colonizer
who brings me coffee
every morning

who grew up
sun-swimming
who knows
how to hold me
when I black out
during intimacy
because I have
forgotten
for a moment
that I am safe

and if I relocate
I will remember
to stop at these trees
will hit the steering wheel
hard and sing

because I will never
be done writing

about old things

Huntress

for Joan Naviyuk Kane on the day we visited
Anne Sexton's grave

beneath a fat gray sky
clouds more threat than snow
did they know
what we would become

to grow the knife
in the belly
the cowering
was a lie
protect the throat
at all costs

a killer whale back home
oil black and bone
was grieving publicly
as she pushed her corpse
calf along the surface
for weeks
death floating
in the Salish Sea

she told her story
again and again
like a poem
you cannot stop speaking

because the spell
isn't working
yet

or was she only waiting
to see who was listening

I am tired of being
misheard

like the photo of a wolf
as she ducks and hovers
at the neck
some part
of her wired
to protect
the mate

the mistake
was in the caption
how the photographer
assumed the other wolf
was male

in a rental car we curve
and twist along the river
the emerald necklace
speeding and dizzy
at the place where
Lady Lazarus
was born

I try not to throw up
because all of it
is overwhelming

in Boston we ghost hunt
get lost in the cemetery
leave a tangle of hair
on a gravestone

and you tell me
we can't end up like this

and I know you're right

because we both paused
at the same time
spoke the words
as we passed it

a tombstone
its carved letters
a spell called
Huntress

Rose Quartz II

To spell
an incantation
is to magic
words into power
to speak them
again and again
is the ancient art
of repetition

I've said my grandmother's name
unnumbered times
have written it into the sand and on the trees
scrawled it along my skin
ingested the lettering

this is for protection
and so my grandmother whispers countercurses
in the language of dreams
remember   red   remember   healing

now in California
along the 101 I ride
with a new beloved

but to fall in love with the girl
is to fall in love with the curse
and I remind him
of his place in all this
that the curse came first

in the redwoods
he makes me coffee
over a fire
and in our circle
of trees I recite
my ghost story

with the flashlight pressed
to my lips
remember this
the day I gave birth
to a fist
full of petals

and even the branches were quiet
had forgotten how to speak
when I showed him the stones
that had become my body
he touched the rose-colored rocks
with his fingers

like he could recognize them
like he understood something
about crystals

we head south
along the coast
I watch ghosts
out the window
we listen to mixtapes
we listen to each other as children

we stop for gas
and for roadside
attractions

a museum of minerals and gems
great halls of geodes
mountains of stacked tourmaline
and we wander past amethyst
and citrine

and it's here along the 101
I find the singing
push open the dusty doors
following

out back are crates of dirt
tools for digging
and miles and miles of rose quartz
stretching fields of pale pink
and I remember the sink
full of roses
the day my body broke

spoke the curse out loud
and dropped to my knees
a group of ancestors
circled the stones
a line of mothers
all singing

one by one
they approached me
each wielding
a silver hammer
to knock the sharp points
from my body

and I watched as they
fell from me into dust
a blush-colored wind
swirling the hot air

I dug the final piece
from my heart
unable to part with it
my grandmother
closed my hand
into a fist

keep this

with you

it is part

of your story

sometimes

to remember

a wound

is the way

of healing

Acknowledgments

Thank you, Jenna, for Coney Island and tarot readings, for the Wonder Wheel and dance parties and the desert. You brought me into that tent and I'm forever grateful.

Thanks to those who showered me in crystal gems and stories of healing.

Rose Quartz would not have been possible without my chosen family, my freaky little coven. Thank you to literally every femme in my life who has nurtured and cared for me when I was falling apart. Your spells, your love, and your playlists of bad '90s pop music held me together, and that's witchcraft.

Thank you to Mary Austin Speaker and Milkweed for believing in these poems and bringing my spells into the world.

Thank you, Joan Naviyuk Kane, for your guidance during my MFA program, when these poems and my spirit were fragile. Thank you for not letting me quit when I wanted to.

Thank you, Ken White, for taking the time to read early drafts and for your honesty, and for Southern California seances in the park.

To the witch who taught me how to read tarot, thank you for showing me how to look closer and how to make choices.

Thank you to the Eight of Swords and The High Priestess.

And thank you, Blaine Slingerland, for being the sun when things went dark, for the ocean and the rose garden, for Santa Cruz and for the legend of how the sun fell in love with the moon.

Bridget McGee Houchins

Sasha taqʷšəblu LaPointe is a Coast Salish author from the Nooksack and Upper Skagit Indian tribes. She received a double MFA in Creative Nonfiction and Poetry from the Institute of American Indian Arts. She lives in Tacoma, Washington.

milkweed
EDITIONS

Founded as a nonprofit organization in 1980, Milkweed Editions
is an independent publisher. Our mission is to identify, nurture,
and publish transformative literature, and build an engaged
community around it.

Milkweed Editions is based in Bdé Óta Othúŋwe (Minneapolis)
within Mní Sota Makhóčhe, the traditional homeland of the
Dakhóta people. Residing here since time immemorial, Dakhóta
people still call Mní Sota Makhóčhe home, with four federally
recognized Dakhóta nations and many more Dakhóta people
residing in what is now the state of Minnesota. Due to continued
legacies of colonization, genocide, and forced removal, generations
of Dakhóta people remain disenfranchised from their traditional
homeland. Presently, Mní Sota Makhóčhe has become a refuge
and home for many Indigenous nations and peoples, including
seven federally recognized Ojibwe nations. We humbly encourage
our readers to reflect upon the historical legacies held in
the lands they occupy.

milkweed.org

Milkweed Editions, an independent nonprofit publisher, gratefully acknowledges sustaining support from our Board of Directors; the Alan B. Slifka Foundation and its president, Riva Ariella Ritvo-Slifka; the Amazon Literary Partnership; the Ballard Spahr Foundation; *Copper Nickel*; the McKnight Foundation; the National Endowment for the Arts; the National Poetry Series; and other generous contributions from foundations, corporations, and individuals. Also, this activity is made possible by the voters of Minnesota through a Minnesota State Arts Board Operating Support grant, thanks to a legislative appropriation from the arts and cultural heritage fund. For a full listing of Milkweed Editions supporters, please visit milkweed.org.

Interior design by Tijqua Daiker and Mary Austin Speaker
Typeset in Baskerville

Baskerville was designed in 1757 by its namesake, John Baskerville.
Created as a part of his larger goal to allow for higher-quality
approaches to industrial book printing, this typeface can be seen as
a bridge between the ornate asymmetrical designs of
the Rococo and the Neoclassical styles.